All Things Bright & Beautiful

A Collection
of Prayer and Verse

Illustrated by
Helen Lanzrein

$\mathcal{T}$hank you, God in heaven,
For a day begun.
Thank you for the breezes,
Thank you for the sun.
For this time of gladness,
For our work and play,
Thank you, God in heaven,
For another day.

Traditional

*F*or this new morning
   and its light,
For rest and shelter
   of the night,
For health and food,
   for love and friends,
For every gift
   your goodness sends,
We thank you,
   gracious Lord.

Anonymous

Dear Father, hear and bless
Thy beasts and singing birds,
And guard with tenderness
Small things that have no words.

Anonymous

Thank you for the beasts so tall,
Thank you for the creatures small,
Thank you for all things that live,
Thank you, God, for all you give.

H. W. Widdows

Our Father, who art in heaven,

Hallowed be thy name.

Thy kingdom come,

Thy will be done,

On earth as it is in heaven.

Give us this day our daily bread,

And forgive us our trespasses,

As we forgive those who

      trespass against us.

And lead us not into temptation,

But deliver us from evil.

For thine is the kingdom,

And the power, and the glory,

For ever and ever.

Amen.

Book of Common Prayer

Father, we thank Thee for this food,
For health and strength and all things good.
May others all these blessings share,
And hearts be grateful everywhere.

Traditional

Please give me what I ask, Dear Lord,
If you'd be glad about it.
But if you think it's not for me
Please help me do without it.

Traditional

*H*e prayeth best, who loveth best
All things both great and small,
For the dear God who loveth us,
He made and loveth all.

Samuel Taylor Coleridge

*B*less this house which is our home.
May we welcome all who come.

Anonymous

For air and sunshine, pure and sweet,
We thank our heavenly Father.
For grass that grows beneath our feet,
We thank our heavenly Father.
For lovely flowers and blossoms gay,
For trees and woods in bright array,
For birds that sing in joyful lay,
We thank our heavenly Father.

Anonymous

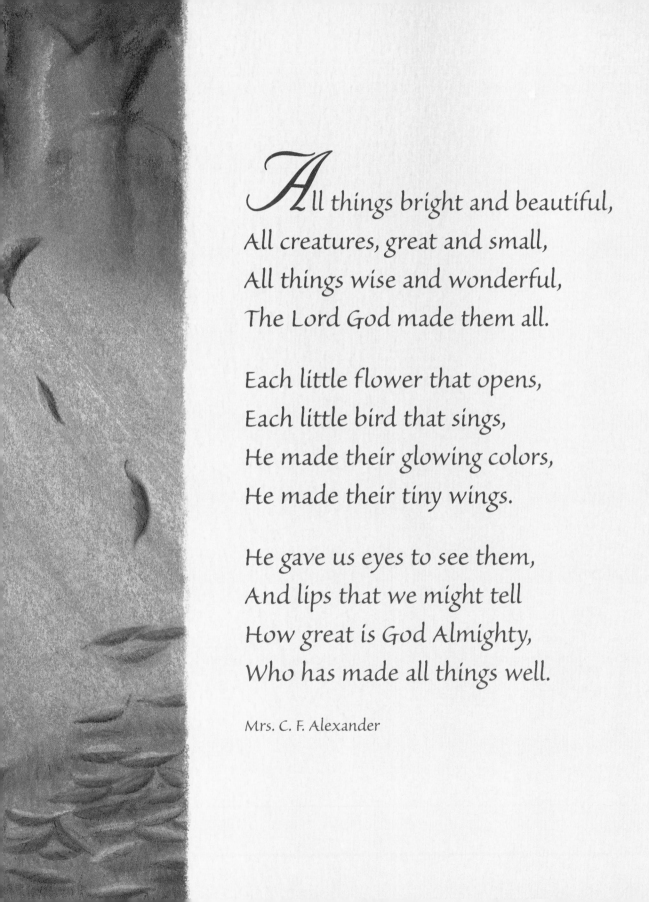

*A*ll things bright and beautiful,
All creatures, great and small,
All things wise and wonderful,
The Lord God made them all.

Each little flower that opens,
Each little bird that sings,
He made their glowing colors,
He made their tiny wings.

He gave us eyes to see them,
And lips that we might tell
How great is God Almighty,
Who has made all things well.

Mrs. C. F. Alexander

*L*ord, keep us safe this night,
Secure from all our fears;
May angels guard us while we sleep,
Till morning light appears.

John Leland

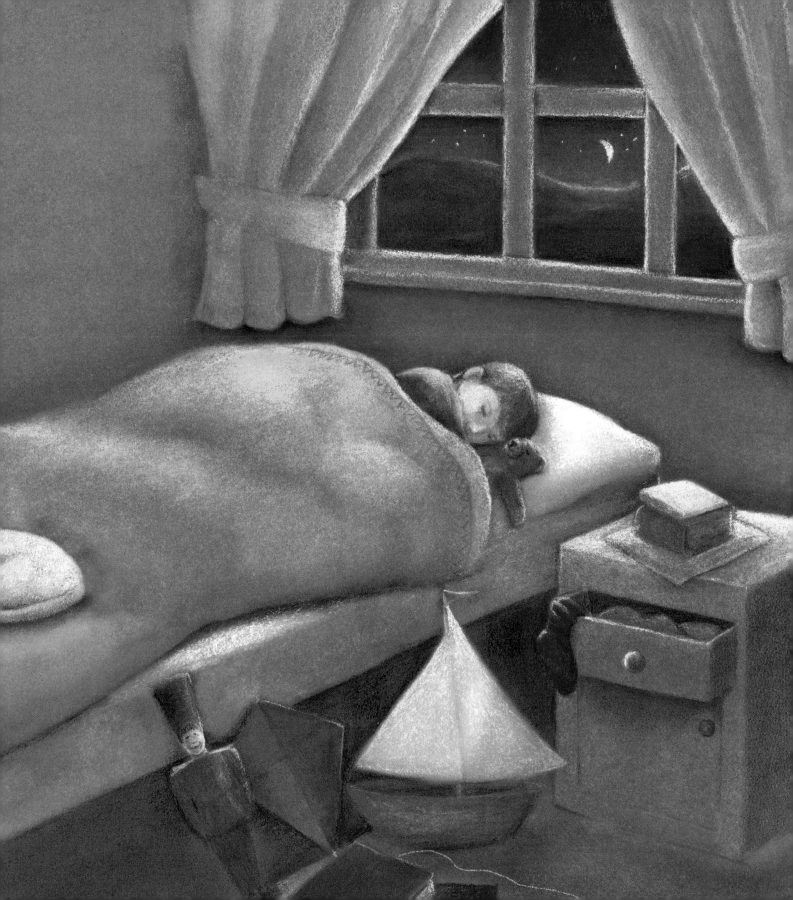

*G*ood night! Good night!
Far flies the light,
But still God's love
Shall flame above,
Making all bright.
Good night! Good night!

Victor Hugo

I see the moon
And the moon sees me.
God bless the moon,
And God bless me.

Anonymous

Day is done,
Gone the sun
From the lake,
From the hills,
From the sky.
Safely rest,
All is well!
God is nigh.

Anonymous

This edition published by Scholastic Inc.,
557 Broadway; New York, NY 10012,
by arrangement with Little Tiger Press.
SCHOLASTIC and associated logos are trademarks and/or
registered trademarks of Scholastic Inc.
Scholastic Canada; Markham, Ontario

Original edition published in English by
Little Tiger Press, an imprint of
Magi Publications, London, England, 2007

Prayer by H. W. Widdows from IN EXCELSIS, compiled
by H. W. Dobson, is used by permission of the National
Society for Promoting Religious Education